These Tattered Wings

Prose and Poetry of a Fractured Girl

By Maya Lee

Photography by David Whipple

If you purchased this book without a cover, you should be aware this book is stolen property the author nor publisher have not received any payment for this "stripped book."

Copyright 2016 by Maya Lee

All rights reserved. No part of this book may be reproduced or transmitted in any form or by electronic or mechanical, including photocopying, recording or any information storage and retrieval system without the written permission of the author, and photographer.

ISBN-13:978-0692723999

ISBN-10:0692723994

First printing May 2016

Cover photograph and photography by David Whipple
www.davidwhipplephotography.com

Acknowledgment and Thanks

To Merri Halma for encouraging me to get this book done.

To David Whipple for supplying the images for this work and for being the best brother, a girl could want.

A very special thank you to my husband Gary. You put up amazingly well with all my melancholic temperaments. I should not forget my In-laws. To my sister-in-law, the floor should be clean soon at least until my next work it due. To my mother-in-law thank you for the smiles every time you see me writing. To my father-in-law, I hope the loud music didn't bother you too much. Thank you to everyone for your support and belief that I could do this.

Table of contents:

These Tattered Wings Part 1 8

Bleeding 11

A Fight for Life 12

These Parts 14

Selling Worlds 17

The Beast 18

You Came 19

Game 21

Departed 22

Beauty Queen 23

These Tattered Wings Part 2 26

Swindle 28

Bitterness 30

Hurt..31

Fractured Girl...33

Boones Farm..36

Infatuation...38

Loss..40

In Want of...41

Pixie...43

Dalliance..44

Mother's Face..46

Oh Mother...48

Inside...49

I'm Blessed..50

Photographs...........................10,16,20,25,29, 32,37,39,42,45,47,51

These Tattered Wings Part 1

Our Screams shatter the night.
We dared to step from the boundaries of birthright.

Darkness folds around me.
Chained and tied, my Wings bound together.
Sentenced to walk alone forever.

Trapped in a body that is no longer my own.
What crime did I commit to be punished so?
This cursed arbitrary punishment they bestow.

Condemned to this world in a mortal shell
with every moment living in pain.
All for the status quo to be maintained.

My soul remembers flying.
The feeling of stretched out wings.
It's torture the way this memory clings.

The feeling of the wind blowing through me.
Why was I left with this remembrance?
Glimpses of freedom, will not bring repentance.

They cast us down and clipped our wings.
Stumbling alone in each life we've lived in.
Separated and wandering, waiting to be forgiven.

A faint remembrance of the light you once had.
Taunts me as we walk the darkness of this land
until we can once again touch hands.

Our wings will grow again no long bound.
Out of the heavens, we were thrown.
Seeking a freedom that we've never known.

We unfairly judged for our violation.
Remember why we won't be forgiven
because love can be a crime in heaven.

Bleeding

My soul lay bleeding,
wounds festered with time.
This soul consumed with needing
the pieces left behind.
A night like any other,
rain-soaked summer ground.
Disappointed by her lover
until she heard a sound.
Not the one she hoped for
a stranger had her bound.
She called out for a savior
but not one could be found.
This lady remembers fondly.
The girl left there to die.
Her strength she trusted blindly
but found it no ally.
She lies there bruised and beaten,
forgotten by her god.
Another angel fallen
to live as human and so flawed.

A Fight for Life

His arm around my neck,
hand clutching my mouth and nose.
No one hears my scream.
My face wet with sweat and rain.
My breath is taken from me.
I fight
This is my life
I'm thrown down
like my body has no weight.
My head smashed upon the ground
but I will not go out.
I will not be broken
This is my life
I taste the blood in my mouth
and the pain in my jaw.
The wounds on my body sting
from the leaves and mud.
I fight
This is my life

No one will save me.
This fight is my own.
I will not die
though I can feel her watching.
My body may be bruised
but you cannot break me.
I fight
This is my life
The blood runs down my face.
I feel my body failing.
My air is running out.
My vision starts to tunnel,
but I don't lose consciousness.
I still fight
This is my life
I may have lost this round
and you have had your way.
You will carry my scars for life
I will remember that you
could not break me
and what I did I did for life.
This is my life
and I will never be broken.

These Parts

Here is my body open and on the table for inspection.
Ready to be labeled for use, duty, and restriction.
All my parts for their purpose, for I can claim no objection.

What parts give me rights and what parts take away?
What parts are strength and what makes me Prey?
What requirements of behavior, for I cannot be risqué?

What about my parts makes my experience invalid?
What aspect makes me naturally weaker and pallid?
Shall my parts make me meek, frigid, or timid?

My life lived questioned as emotional bias.
My parts judged, then given instruction by the callous.
and if my voice disagrees I'm deemed impious.

Wisdom gained, brushed aside as hormonal hysterics.
As if my thoughts are poison and caustic.
These views on my parts are indeed prehistoric.

Why is my value as a life judged upon these parts?
What invaluable knowledge gives you right to judge my parts.
Assuming that one knows what's right and wrong about parts

To mark my parts, to pass laws upon my parts,
enforce how I can care for and defend my parts,
and dictate how I must use my parts.

What about my parts makes me unable to decide?
That so many restrictions must be applied.
Do my parts in any way truly hurt your pride?

Why must your judgment of these parts be public stage?
By a council of men well past old age
and others whom from realities of life are disengaged.

Why are my parts national debate?
How do these parts determine my souls mate?
Your reasoning's never do equate.

What about these parts, has you spun so tight?
That you claim to know what is wrong and right.
Your arguments are weak and hateful trite!

Change your view I'm not the whore.
What did you sell, for that seat you scored?
Where you sit and tell me what my parts are for.

Selling Worlds

What would you sell me,
with my pocket full of change?
Your plastic has rejected me,
as I stand in this world
of artificial fantasy.

Where no man works his scrap of soil,
to feed his unending hungers.
Starving souls push buttons,
selling curios of desire
and satisfactions merely temporal.

Starvation through indulgences,
pestilence in the cures,
war with lies of freedom.
Eating whatever you are served.
Blinded in folly and lead by arrogance.

Chew on rocks to devour the world.
Foolish endeavors of kings and knaves
in the name of faceless gods.
Blameless are the hungry masses,
for their voices remain unheard.

The Beast

A beast with no form stalks the night.
Its growls cannot be heard.
It devours soul that memories haunt.
Seeking what's been fractured.

A little crack is all it needs.
A sliver to inhabit.
With teeth and claws, it digs right in
and feasts upon the spirit.

You Came

I leave before your feet this dead bird within my head.
This victim of a soul's starvation has become my daily bread.

Left lonely and aching for vengeance, my broken heart.
Pushed to the side like a broken doll and her shattered parts.

Halfhearted promises filled this girl with lovely daydreams.
Now reality leaves me choking down my muffled screams.

I was just a broken doll, lost with no one who cared.
You came to me honestly with your flaws plainly bared.

We eyed each other's scars from battles wished forgotten,
and shared our stories of the life we had been caught in.

Your touch brushed away the cobwebs from my skin.
You never spewed out declarations of endless love or sin.

You simply caressed my cheek and wipe away my lonely tears.
Never judging my unhinged soul beset with unnamed fears.

You held me within your gentle arms like I was new
and gave me a love that I could finally live through.

Game

Self-destruction is a game I play.
My own mortality on display.
Weakness embedded in my sinew.
Waiting for its next venue
to play, it's game of desecration.
From its curse, I seek liberation.
Now it calls, the time is here.
Don't let this be the time I disappear.

Departed

I no longer wish to live with memories.
We all die in time, crossing to the other lands.
Each sent to that river to meet our ferries.

I've known many who've past before.
Four who've fallen by their own hand.
A brother fell with his final score.

Weakness of body took another.
One was lost in the name of war.
A future sister murdered by her mother.

My uncle that I held so dear,
lived life fully and passed with age.
So many more that I picture clear.

These memories are haunting me.
I feel their loss with each passing year,
and wonder if the pain is jealousy.

Beauty Queen

Such a foolish girl, to want more than you are worth.
Hiding your misery with intolerable mirth.

You're a broken thing, tied down by an unending curse.
No amount of fooling yourself will make it disperse.

You know better than to spread your taint.
You drag them down with your lack of restraint.

What of those things that swim in your head?
Things that go unanswered, the things that you dread.

If they knew what laid behind that plastered on smile,
that foolish mask of wit and guile.

The unclean
The unforeseen
The fractured beauty queen

Would you impersonate the victim in the end?
The innocent, who no one would stand up to defend.

The secret is that you're out of your head.
The fear that your eulogy will go unread.

No one to remember your failed ascent.
Your soul void of any true intent.

Vacant of truth, the love you feign.
False blessings of a lover's pain.

Draining loves breath with your cursed kiss.
You can't change yourself with an empty wish.

The frost of winter lays within your breast.
The coldest heart of this unwanted guest.

These Tattered Wings Part 2

How could you forget what came before?
So soft, your touch is like the anticipation of sunset.
I see your shadow creep and I know.
You have come to hurt me once again.
I heard the lure of your bitter dirge.
Whispering temptation and yearned for words.
" Come into the darkness, my broken little angel
You're trapped in fear at the coming of twilight.
How can I release you from the chains you bind yourself in?"
Curled up like an infant in your arms.
Feeling like I've known you for so long.
Your touch, crawl under my skin.
I said the words I should never have been spoken.
Slipping out from me without thought or consideration
To those words of love, all you could do was sneer.
You treat me as original sin, a forbidden fruit.
Tempting out the weakness in you.
I just wanted to hold you once again
but you only play at pulling out my feathers.
I was never what you thought I was.
My wings far from a pristine splendor.

I let you put the blame on me
for your fall from grace and love.
You never knew what you had in me
but I'll be who is sorry in the end.
This temptation into self-destruction
I couldn't help but listen to your words.
I threw it away to taste the forbidden
and now the sky is out of reach.
I've grown a little cold inside
Every day you are no longer near.
Without a word of where you went
I'm left with my memories here
May I forget your stolen kisses
that still linger on these dreadful lips.
Give me back my broken wings.
So, I may fly away from this misery you left me in
May I forget, May I forget!
The way your scent lingered
with me along in this abyss.
I don't need you coming back
astride your white horse and stolen wings.
Don't return to me with fairytale promises.
I will not be your princess in distress.
I do not need to be saved by you.
I do not want to be taken to you liars' kingdom.

Swindle

Sharp tongue that speaks that lie of it.
Wanton women spread their slit.
Once part of a darker world.
The bitch that pays back tenfold.
Sit watching as dreams dwindle,
knowing out of your love swindled.

Bitterness

You make my palms sweat.
My racing heart skips a beat.
I begin to melt into you,
fearing what you may be.

Lost in your eyes,
staring into this dream.
I hold to a fleeting connection
accepting it to be all we have.

A moment in your arms.
Then you are done with me,
or I grow weary of you.
This is the bitterness of love

A moment of reckless passion
to rip out an enamored soul.
Then moving on to another
to excitedly replay the pain again.

Hurt

Do you know how bad it hurts
that you don't lust for me?
I want your love, I want your desire,
I want to feel you burn in me.
Set my body afire!
I want your soul to devour,
to have your breath in me.
Filling my lungs with your power.
You took my best and now I sit
empty to the core of me.
Still unable, to my fate submit.
Your inconvenient pet,
wishing you to notice me.
The one so easy to forget.
You make me want to hurt myself
with the way, you do not see me.
Leaving me to wait on the shelf
unwanted, weeping, and hollow.
That is the fate for me
an empty doll, forever shallow.
Clawing at my wasted skin.
It has no use for me,
it's grown too thin.

Fractured Girl

Poor fractured little doll,
wanting love only to fall.

Disappointed by your married bliss.
How could you want even more than this?

Just because he said forever,
does not make him your source of pleasures.

So, shut those legs he won't want you either.
A desperate little whore with a fever.

Poor little-broken doll,
a victim of a tragic fall.

You've forgotten ledges are so steep.
All while thinking that you were, oh so deep.

In your dance, you took that step.
Thinking all who saw were in your debt.

All it took was a little slip.
Over the edge, you took your dip.

Have you forgotten you're just a doll?
Nothing more, that is all.

Do you really think you are worth it?
No one wants to be dragged into your pit.

Look at you now, you little brat.
Rejected again didn't think of that.

The one who spoke that vow,
really doesn't want you now.

Pathetic waiting on the fantasy of love.
Just wait till reality gives you a shove.

Saying stupid things like he would care.
Self-destruction your dance of despair.

What's left when you remove the seventh veil?
All those dreams start to derail.

No more teasing he'll see what is real
and who you are could break the deal.

He wants more than a dancing poppet
and there's nothing you can do to stop it.

So back onto the shelf never to be touched.
A broken doll in an old china hutch.

You flirt, you tease
but who do you please?

Always trying to fill that hole
but chasing after air has taken its toll.

Open wounds of a bleeding tart,
drip infection from your tainted heart.

Boones Farm

Boones farm at seventeen,
summer nights and teenage dreams.

In monsoon heat, and India ink.
Blood stains cover up the pink.

Wishing to be one of the guys,
but judged by what's between her thighs.

Bruises blushed before flowers.
Pulled apart by other powers.

Playing at identities game.
A fractured girl will not tame.

Infatuation

Suffocating that pain deep within my breast.
Forced denial of myself,
pulled by the undertow of past regret.

The longing stirred within my chest.
While stuck in emotional purgatory.
Not knowing if you will see, what I want to forget.

Poisoned by yearnings from my space below.
Denied that urge that would break our faith.
Twisting of desires within my guts.

On dangerous grounds, I navigate slow.
Never let known that internal burning.
That transgression would be the deepest of cuts.

This is only a crush,
I do not need to feel your touch.
I don't need to feel your breath on my neck.

This is a little infatuation.
No need to make it a situation.
For you, my life I will not wreck.

Loss

A shiver runs through me.
My breath grows shallow.
I can feel you.
Remember what you smelt like.
The way you tasted.
I can see every move.
Every curve of your body.
The glisten of sweat on your chest.
The way your beating heart sounded.
How cruel of life to bring you to me,
then tell me I can't have you.

In Want of

I love infatuation!

That single heart beat and flush of skin,

when the thoughts pour in.

Thump! Thump! Thump!

You relive that first moment of connection.

and they way their touch was perfection

Again and Again!

The ache from between your breast,

becomes the sweetest invited guest.

Flesh to Flesh!

Those memories you wish to haunt

and you know, just what you want.

Dalliance

To crawl inside and find the warmth,
the simplest desire of human flesh.
Seeking a truth in ever dalliance.
Finding souls that to not mesh.

So, we etch the world upon our skin.
Wearing shields of heart and stone,
to mask our fears and grace.
All that posturing keeps us alone.

I taste sweet like the smell of summer.
I'll be temptation in musky heat.
Taking you past your paper walls,
to the place where two souls meet.

Take my hand and we will go beyond.
This shell we wear so tight.
Enter me and will you see,
that even in darkness there is light.

Pixie

There is a pixie in me.

She loves the wind and loves to play.

The spark of life is her game.

Come and dally with this Fay

and your life will never be the same.

Mother's faces

Sati you were created for temptation.

To lure Shiva from his mountain isolation.

As Uma, you were for him a love innocent and sweet.

As Paravati, he persuaded you to take the bride's seat.

As Kali, you trampled Shiva at your feet.

As Uma, in shame, you took your own breath.

As Paravati, you became the mother of Ganesh.

As Kali, you are the end and ego's death.

Oh Mother

Oh, Mother open your golden arms.
Show this lost child the path they must take.
Oh, mother open your heart
and lead me through the muddy swamp.

Guard me against the darkness,
that lies in wait beneath the pools.
Let me not be lost in the waves of Maya,
blinding my eyes and drowning my soul.

Inside

Like any girl, she searched to find,
that little place inside her mind.
Away from the judgment of another,
that place inside where she is no other.
The place where she is the self-whole,
that place where she can touch her soul.
There's the strength she cannot hide,
the power of self found deep inside.

I'm Blessed

I've tasted sorrows, that poison souls.
Seen into the darkness that takes steep tolls.
I've felt the pain in others eyes
and failed to see past a monster's disguise.
I have been a failure to others and experienced the same.
I've seen suffering in action and chosen to take blame.
I have spoken lies to hide my truth
and all the mistakes of an ill-spent youth.
Gave into impulse and have broken love.
I've done so many things to be ashamed of.
I've learned a secret upon this path.
I've seen things change in the aftermath.
A world beyond the great abstract.
I now know, evolution as a fact.

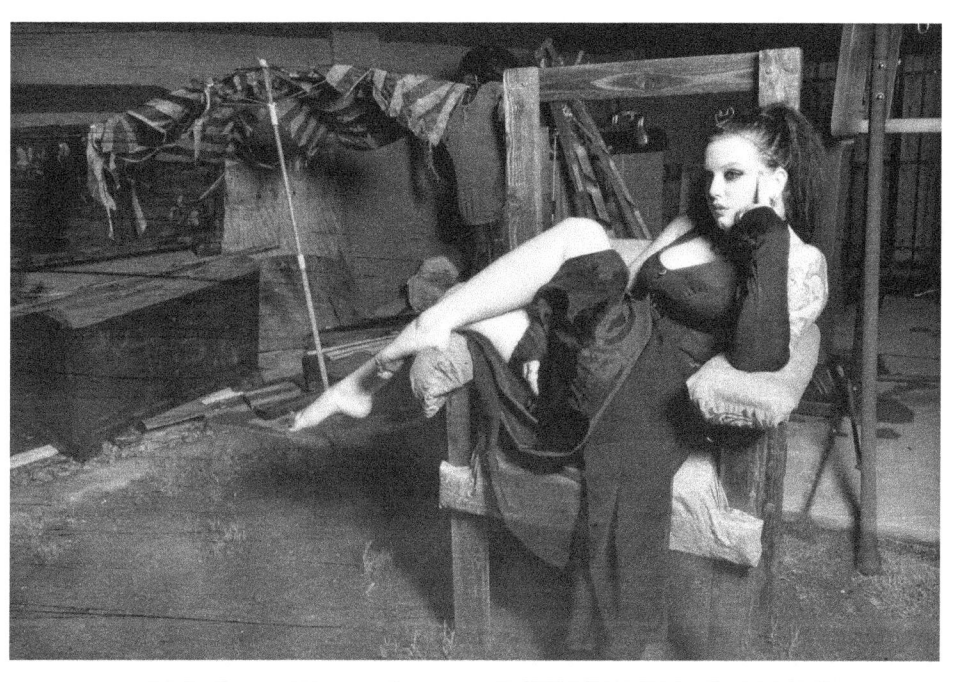

www.ingramcontent.com/pod-product-compliance
Lightning Source LLC
Chambersburg PA
CBHW031505040426
42444CB00007B/1212